Giggle Belly

By Page Sakelaris

Illustrated by Richard L. Torrey

SCHOLASTIC INC.

New York Toronto London Auckland Sydney
Mexico City New Delhi Hong Kong Buenos Aires

For Isabelle, Bennet, and their Daddy. You make my belly giggle.
—P. S.

To Sue, Heather, and Drew.
—R. L. T.

Reading Consultants
Linda Cornwell
Coordinator of School Quality and Professional Improvement
(Indiana State Teachers Association)

Katharine A. Kane
Education Consultant
(Retired, San Diego County Office of Education and San Diego State University)

ISBN 0-516-24134-6

12 11 10 9 8 7 6 5 4   7/0

Printed in the United States of America.   08

First Scholastic printing, April 2002

There's a giggle in my belly,

and a tickle in my toes,

a wave of my arms,
and an itch
on my nose,

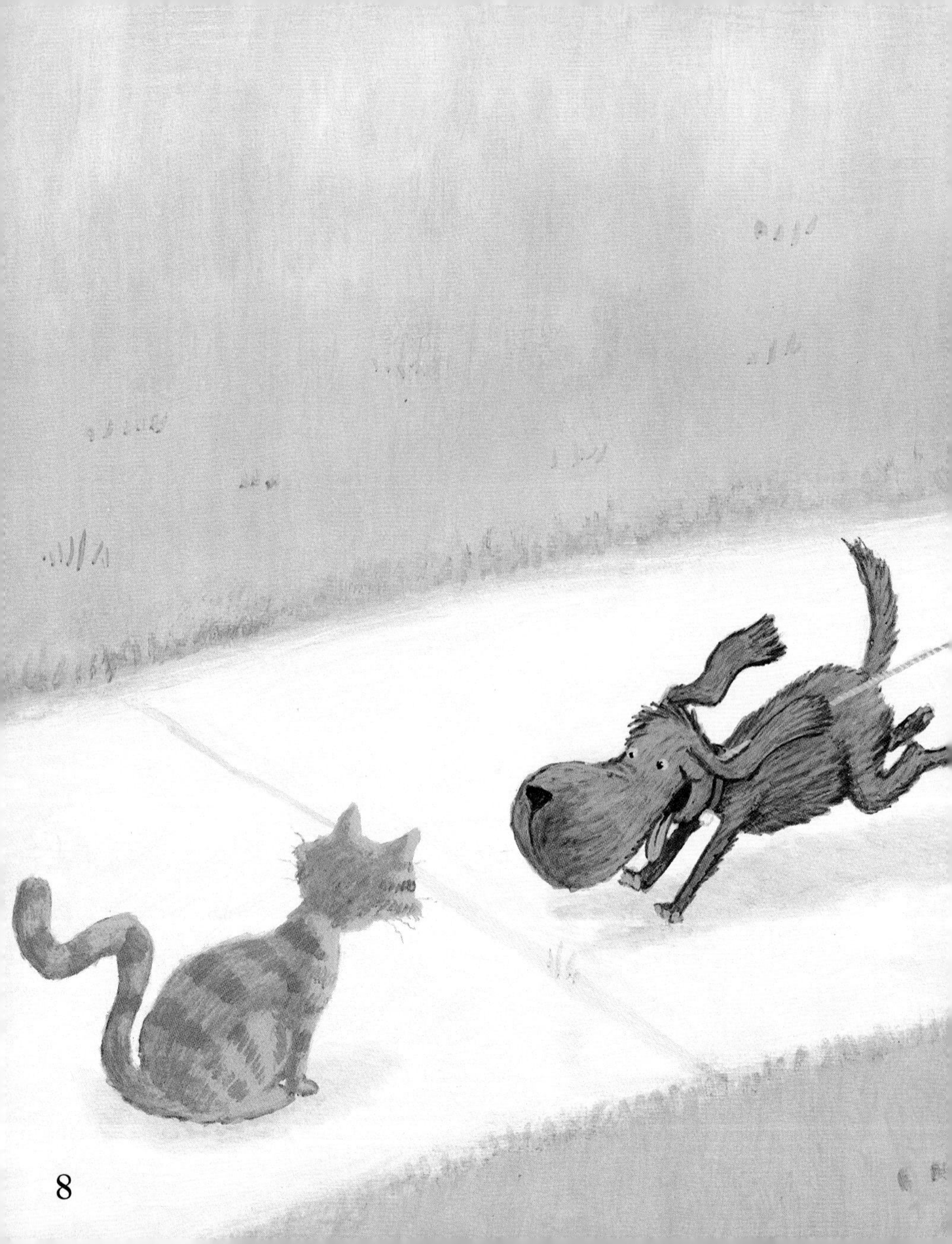

a twist in my waist,

a swing in my shin,

a snap in my fingers,
and a grin above my chin.

There's a nod of my head,

a tug of my ear,

a hop in my feet,

and a bend right here.

There's a swallow in my throat,

a stroke of my hair,

a clap of my hands,
and a shimmy everywhere.

There's a wink in my eye,

a kiss on my lips,

a shrug of my shoulders,

and a wiggle in my hips.

Word List (50 words)

a	fingers	my	swing
above	giggle	nod	there's
an	grin	nose	throat
and	hair	of	tickle
arms	hands	on	toes
belly	head	right	tug
bend	here	shimmy	twist
chin	hips	shin	waist
clap	hop	shoulders	wave
ear	in	shrug	wiggle
everywhere	itch	snap	wink
eye	kiss	stroke	
feet	lips	swallow	

About the Author

Page Sakelaris lives in University Park, Texas, with her husband, Jim, their two-year-old twins, Isabelle and Bennet, and their tremendous white dog, Rooney. The whole family takes Rooney for long walks nearly every evening. Page loves just being with her family, reading to her children, and telling funny stories.

About the Illustrator

Richard Torrey's illustrations and cartoons have appeared in newspapers and magazines all over the world. He is a two-time syndicated cartoonist and the designer of a large line of greeting cards. This is the seventh children's book Richard has illustrated. He lives in Long Island, New York, with his wife, Sue, and his children, Heather and Drew.